Preface

I was never taught finance: saving, investing, protecting wealth. The education system failed to teach me, and my kids, how to manage money. Luckily, I have always been a saver, but I knew nothing about investing; investing was not for the likes of me (except luckily through my pension pot and later an ISA). In my pursuit to understand investing, I found 3 simple steps to becoming wealthy that I wanted to teach to my children. This was the genesis of my book.

Three years ago, at the age of 52, I was made redundant. Not knowing if I would be able to get another job, or whether I actually wanted one, I decided to find out whether my nest egg would be enough to live on, indefinitely. This was the start of my financial journey.

I knew how to save, but I was afraid to tackle investing on my own. My first thought was that I would need a financial adviser, but trying to pick one was very complicated: what would they do? what would they charge? how would they help me? They seemed to be offering to manage my money for a fee – which was not what I wanted. I carried on researching and reading everything I could find about investing.

It soon became very clear, that over the last decade, the investment world has changed significantly, and now everybody has access to wealth creation tools that only the wealthy had access to in the past. It is now significantly easier to 'Do It Yourself' without the need for a financial adviser.

I can do it myself, so can my children, and so can you! It's easy!
With a few simple changes to my nest egg, I am F.I.R.E.
We are not rich, but I now know how to budget and manage money effectively. If I started again today, following the 3 simple steps to becoming wealthy, I would have been rich by now.

The book is split into two parts. Part one explains exactly what you need to do to become wealthy. Part two goes into more detail explaining why and what you are doing - if you want to know more. My kids have found it simple, easy to understand, and indispensable - I hope you find the same!

DAVID GRIFFIN
david.griffintstfs@gmail.com

Copyright © 2021 David Griffin
All rights reserved.

This book is for education. Whilst every effort has been made to ensure that information in this book is accurate, no liability can be accepted for any loss incurred in any way whatsoever by any person relying solely on the information contained herein.

Content

PART ONE
- SAVE – Spend less than you earn, pay yourself first & automate.
    - BUDGET
    - EMERGENCY FUND
    - SPENDING: LIFESTYLE CREEP AND THE LATTE FACTOR
    - DEBT
    - SAVVY SHOPPING
    - PASSIVE INCOME
- INVEST – Be effective, keeping costs and tax low.
    - THE POWER OF THREE: ISA   LISA   PENSION
    - IT'S ALL ABOUT THE MAGIC OF COMPOUND INTEREST
    - WHAT IS INVESTING
    - WHERE TO INVEST
    - HOW TO INVEST
    - THE F.I.R.E MOVEMENT
- PROTECT – Your family & your wealth.
- Success with money can be guaranteed.

PART TWO
- It is not *"All about the money, money, money!"*
- Behavioural finance and investor bias
- Pension V ISA
- Passive investing
- Target Date Retirement funds
- Fixed ratio Equity:Bond funds
- What is the best balance of Equities and Bonds
- Passive investing does not have to be complicated
- Passive investing can be complicated, if you want!
- Bucket structure for F.I.
- Financial plan
- Practical example
- And finally….

Financial success is guaranteed if you follow three simple steps:

1. SAVE - Spend less than you earn, pay yourself first & automate.

2. INVEST - Be effective, keeping costs and tax low.

3. PROTECT- Your family & your wealth.

SAVE – Spend less than you earn, pay yourself first & automate

All saving/investing needs to be automated or it won't happen. Once done, very rarely missed.

This Builds Wealth!   Automate your way to wealth!

To help you spend less than you earn you can use the 50/30/20 rule as a starting point, but you should adapt the final budget to your lifestyle and income. The 50/30/20 Income rule:

1. 50% of your income should cover essentials (rent, utilities, groceries, petrol, etc.).
2. 30% of your income covers none essentials/discretionary spending (eating out, holidays, gym, fun, etc.).
3. 20% save/invest. This is you paying your future self. Your future self will be grateful!

Saving at least 20% of your income and paying yourself first, every month, automatically by Direct Debit. I cannot stress enough……… …..This Will Make You WEALTHY!

Saving is easiest to do when you first start earning and begin straight away; you won't even miss it. It becomes more difficult later on due to 'lifestyle creep'. If you can't start with 20% then just start with 5%……..anything!………..then increase over time.

BUDGET

Nobody likes to budget, but in the real world, the only way to ensure you spend less than you earn is to know your **written** budget. There are numerous budgeting Apps available (many linked to bank accounts) which you may find are the best way forward for you.

But to keep it simple, if you know your monthly essential costs (i.e. the 50%), most of which are paid monthly by direct debit; and you are paying yourself first (i.e. the 20%), saving automatically by direct debit, then you know how much discretionary spend you have without any in-depth need to budget.

Simples!

Where is all the money going?!   Keep a simple spreadsheet:

INCOME each month (ie take home cash)	£2,600		INCOME PER ANNUM (ie take home cash)	£31,200
ESSENTIALS (Fixed Monthly DD's)			ESSENTIALS (Annual Costs)	
MORTGAGE	£300		Home Insurance	£300
COUNCIL TAX	£200		Car Insurance x 2	£500
ELECT/GAS	£100		car service/MOT/Tax	£400
CAR PCP	£200		Xmas/Birthdays	£400
TV/BROADBAND/TV LICENCE	£100		Dentist	£100
WATER	£40		Petrol worked out at pa	£500
MOBILE PHONE	£10		Food worked out at pa	£5,200
CHARITY	£100		Holidays x 2 worked out at	£3,000
TOTAL PER MONTH	£1,050		TOTAL PER MONTH	£867
TOTAL PER ANNUM	£12,600		TOTAL PER ANNUM	£10,400
Total Essentials per annum	£23,000		If your essential costs are greater than 50%, first try to reduce them with alternatives. Otherwise, you will have to take from your non-essentials or savings. The choice is yours.	
Total as a % of income	74%			
Total Savings per annum	£6,000			
Total as a % of income	19%			
Discretionary Spend per anum	£2,200			
Discretionary Spend per month	£180			

The spreadsheet shows monthly essentials on the left (£1,050 per month), and annual essentials on the right (£10,400 per annum which breaks down to £876 per month).
All monthly essentials should be paid by direct debit directly from the bank current account that your income is paid into.
The annual essentials which are budgeted for at a total of £867 per month, can either be left in the current account or moved to a savings account.

Wait….are holidays, Xmas, Sky TV, mobile phones all essentials!? Yes…and No. Beware 'Lifestyle Creep'. If you are spending 'intentionally', there will always be a cross over between what is deemed essential and none essential – it depends on you, as does the level of savings you are prepared to make.

The spreadsheet shows that this person has decided to save £6,000 per annum, or £500 per month.
Money for savings/investments goes from the bank current account that your income is paid into, to alternative accounts **by direct debit at the start of every month**.

Don't save what's left over after spending. Spend what's left over after saving. Pay yourself first!

The spreadsheet shows that money left over for none essentials come to £2,200 per annum or £180 per month. This should be moved to a contact card account for daily spending.
If you use a credit card for daily spending, then pay for the credit card in full by monthly direct debit from this card.

Food and petrol are included in the spreadsheet as estimated annual essentials as the amount will vary from week to week and cannot be paid through direct debit. By reviewing past spending, it has been estimated that £5,700 per annum, or £475 per month, will be spent on food and petrol. This should also be transferred to the contact card account on a monthly basis.

All you now need to do is make sure the contact card account is spent throughout the month and doesn't run dry.
If you are using a credit card in tandem, allow for this spend too (this involves more control).
If you underspend some months, great, this will build up a buffer for seasonal variations and bigger lifestyle spends e.g. a new phone.

Always check your accounts regularly: do a direct debit audit every month to ensure the correct amounts are coming out!

EMERGENCY FUND

Before you start saving/investing for the long term, create an emergency fund of at least 3-6 months' living expenses; you never know what's around the corner (Covid!). This fund will stop you from going into debt if something unplanned happens.
Keep this in a savings account or premium bonds for quick and easy access.

Deciding how much you need is a bit like deciding on the length of a piece of string - decide what is right for you. You might want to put some money aside each month for big lifestyle spends, like a special holiday or a car, etc.

SPENDING: LIFESTYLE CREEP AND THE LATTE FACTOR

When you first start full-time work, you will have more money than you ever had before! Enjoy life and follow these simple rules to gain financial success!

Spend **intentionally**. Determine what makes you the happiest and then plan your finances so that you can afford this lifestyle. Spend less than you earn and control costs to enjoy better holidays, great nights out, or whatever you enjoy doing!

Learn the pleasure of delayed gratification. Delay reward in the short term in order to enjoy greater rewards in the long term.

When you get a pay rise or bonus, keep to the above…..or stick it all in savings as you won't miss it!

Watch out for 'Lifestyle Creep'. Lifestyle creep occurs when your standard of living improves as your discretionary income rises and former luxuries become new necessities.

No income is big enough if you can't live within your means. Robert De Nero recently admitted he was broke, even after earning millions each year!

It isn't about being frugal or tight, it's about spending intentionally. If you enjoy that £3.50 latte on the way to work each morning, or that M&S lunch, etc., fair enough, so be it! That is your choice and is intentional. But, could you have coffee at work for free, cheaper brands, or take a packed lunch???
These are small examples of Lifestyle Creep; more costly examples would be a bigger car, better holiday, expensive phone, etc. These are OK if you have chosen to spend **intentionally**!

The Latte Factor concept is simple. Small amounts of money spent on a regular basis **unintentionally** cost us far more than we can imagine. The Latte Factor isn't about latte; it's about any seemingly trivial discretionary expense we incur unintentionally.

But take the daily latte as an example. By cutting this out, you will save £3.50 a day, that's £75 per month. If you were to save this, set up a monthly DD into an Equity ISA paying 5% pa, by the time you retire you would have……..£115,000!

If you were to put this into your pension, with tax back and employer contribution, by the time you retire you would have……..£287,000!

One latte a day! Small amounts matter. It is easier today to spend than ever before….but it is also easier to track your spending. Track your expenses for a week and find your 'latte factor'.

Some dismiss the Latte Factor because they want to "enjoy life", "life is short" and we must "live for the day." These clichés certainly have some truth. Yet rarely do I hear people say, "Life is short, I'm going to read a good book" or "Life is short, I'm going to spend time with family." For some reason, these clichés are always used to justify spending money. Here's the point. We spend money on stuff that doesn't make us happy. It may give us some immediate gratification, but no lasting joy. If we ran an experiment and shunned our "latte" for 21 days, I think we'd find that we didn't miss it at all. That's true whether we are talking about a cup of coffee, a new shiny pc, or a new car.

Mow your own lawn. Clean your own car/house. Make a packed lunch (tastes better too!). Don't try to "keep up with the Jones'".

DEBT

Don't have any bad debt!
Good debt is OK e.g. student loan, mortgage, and car PCP (..?).

Before you start saving and investing, pay off bad debt first.
Remember debt **compounds** too! (See later section).

When you take out a mortgage, the higher the loan to value LTV, the lower the interest rate you will pay i.e. the bigger the deposit – the smaller the interest rate.
To get the best mortgage deal, do your own research, and then visit a mortgage broker.

A credit card can be a useful tool. Used carefully, it can help you manage your finances, and build your credit score.

There's very little chance you'll be able to live your life without borrowing money at any point – whether it's for university, a house or something else that you need. Logic has changed over the years. While our grandparents may say "don't ever borrow" this is no longer feasible. We now live in a different world and so need to be equipped with the tools that work. Get debt wrong and it'll cost you a fortune. Unlike most other things we spend cash on, you can't cancel your debts, so you need to get it right first time. More people lead miserable lives because of debt than any other single factor.
Credit cards do NOT give you free money! You have to pay back every penny you spend......AND A WHOLE LOT MORE. Interest charges on credit cards can be EXTREME!
Credit cards cost you nothing as long as you pay off all the balance each month IN FULL! (Set up a direct debit to do this and you never pay any interest!)

Martin Lewis

Should I pay off my mortgage?

Psychologically you may feel it is beneficial to pay off your mortgage, but financially first consider which would make you more money? For example, if your mortgage interest rate is 2% and you can earn 4% by saving/investing then the smart thing to do is keep the money working for you. This is called **leverage**.

SAVVY SHOPPING

The internet has changed the way we buy everything and there are many tools that offer to help you make the best choice. Websites that can quickly search the web to find you the cheapest price, or the best quality product. Others that can offer additional discounts buying through them.

ALWAYS REFER TO MONEYSAVINGEXPERT BEFORE BUYING ANYTHING AND USE COMPARISON WEBSITES.

LOYALTY IS NEVER REWARDED! What you will usually get, if you are loyal to a company, is a bad deal. Companies are not your friends. By staying with the same company – whether it's a bank, an insurance firm, or even your mobile phone provider - you will pay more!

Home insurance/Car insurance: always get quotes from comparison sites between 20-24 days before the renewal date as this can save £100's! Only pay monthly if the interest rate is negligible.

Martin Lewis Money Mantra: Do I need it? Is it worth it? Have I checked if it's cheaper elsewhere? If not...Don't buy it.

PASSIVE INCOME

So far, we have discussed spending less than you earn. You earn a salary, lower expenses by budgeting and watching how you spend, and save as much as possible.

You can speed this up by earning more, either by moving jobs for more salary or through additional part-time employment.

Alternatively, try to build a **passive income** - deploy time and/or money to develop something that will then deliver income with little further work. You can build passive income using 3 key asset classes:

- Business - Working in your own business, part-time or full time, is the traditional route to wealth. If you are happy in an employed role, you can develop additional income through 'side hustles'. For example; sell an eBook online, selling stock photos, create an App, create a Utube channel, write a blog, design T-Shirts....etc. Aim to develop an appreciating asset.

- Property - Buy a rental property and enjoy the rent as passive income.

- Investing - Investing is a great example of passive income. You invest money in a company stock, and then you receive a dividend payment **and** appreciation on the investment without having to do anything at all!

INVEST – Be effective, keeping costs and tax low

THE POWER OF THREE: ISA   LISA   PENSION

For most of us, Pensions and ISAs are all we need to build wealth. There is so much flexibility in these accounts that you are unlikely to need anything else. These accounts are simply 'wrappers with tax benefits' for saving and investing.

ISA (Individual Savings Account):
All payments made into an ISA can be withdrawn at any time without any tax liability. Normal savings accounts and general investment accounts both attract tax.

LISA (Lifetime ISA):
A special ISA. You can pay up to £4,000 into a LISA each year and the government will give you a 25% bonus i.e. £1,000!

FREE MONEY to Compound!

This can only be used to buy a house or as a pension, otherwise, withdrawals have penalties. No brainer if you are buying a house!

For buying a house, use a *savings* LISA - short term saving, lower potential returns but less volatility.
For pension saving, use an *Investment* LISA - longer term saving, higher potential returns but greater volatility.

With a LISA, unlike a pension, all withdrawals can be taken from the age of 60 free of income tax!

You can pay a maximum of £20,000 each year into a Lisa and ISA in total.

Pension (Company or Personal Pension Scheme):

If your employer has a Company Pension Scheme, they will usually make a contribution matching what you pay e.g. if you pay £100 a month, your employer gives you £100 as well. This is in addition to your agreed salary!

FREE MONEY to Compound! Make sure you max this out!

If your employer does not provide a company pension scheme, you will have to find a platform like Vanguard to provide a Personal Pension (also known as a SIPP: Self Invested Personal Pension).

All payments into pensions are tax-free and the government will give you a 25% bonus. If you pay £100 into your pension, the government also pays £25 into your pension.

FREE MONEY to Compound!

Withdrawals from pensions cannot be taken until age 55 and are taxed as income (25% can be withdrawn tax-free).

NOTE: the above is not *The State Pension* which is provided to everybody by the government, the amount of which is dependent on the number of year's national insurance tax you have paid.

IT'S ALL ABOUT THE MAGIC OF COMPOUND INTEREST: EINSTEIN CALLED THIS "THE EIGHTH WONDER OF THE WORLD!"

Compound interest is basically about earning interest on your interest. The earlier you start, the more interest you can earn on your interest, on your interest, on your interest, on your interest...!

For example, let's say that today you (as a 20 something-year-old) invest £10,000 and don't touch it until you retire. Assuming a 6% return on that investment:

- At retirement it will be worth £129,854.
- If the investment is delayed by ten years, the end sum will be £76,860.
- If the investment is delayed by 20 years, the end sum will be just £42,918!

Warren Buffet: "Going from £0 to £100k is the hardest part. After this, compound interest does the hard work".

The rule of 72 is generally used to determine how long it would take for an investment to double given the annual rate of return. At a 6% compound growth rate, it will take just 12 years for the portfolio to double (72/6=12 years).

How to become a millionaire using the power of compound interest!:

If a 20 year old invests £190 per month in the FTSE100, based on historical figures, that 20 year old will retire with £1 Million.

If the £190 per month is increased each year in line with inflation, this will be a 'real value' £1 Million.

If the payment is made into a company pension and matched by the employer, to retire with £1 Million, the 20 year old only has to pay just £76 per month!!

Do not underestimate the power of compound interest and the value of starting early:

£1,000 invested at 10% compound interest after 1 year = £110
After 2 years = £1,210
After 3 years = £1,331
After 4 years = £1,464
After 5 years = £1,610
After 6 years = £1,771
After 7 years = £1,949 Nearly doubled.
After 10 years = £2,594
After 15 years = £4,177 Quadrupled.
After 20 years = £6,727
After 25 years = £10,834 Times 10.
After 30 years = £17,449
After 35 years = £28,100
After 40 years = £45,260 More than £1,000 added each year.

WHAT IS INVESTING

Saving usually means putting your money into cash products, such as a savings account in a bank or building society. Saving typically allows you to earn a low return but with virtually no risk.

Investing is taking some of your money and trying to make it grow by buying things you think will increase in value over the long term. For example, you might invest in equity, property, or buy into an investment fund. Investing allows you to earn a higher return, but you take on the risk of loss in order to do so. Investing is 'buy and hold'- 'stay the course'! You only lose if you sell when the market is down. Controlled behaviour through all market cycles.

Speculating is different to investing. Speculating/trading/gambling is buying one company share or one sector of the market and hoping it goes up in the short term.

"From the moment we're numerate – we go to school and learn maths, we become adults and read the news – we are taught that risk is in the stock market and that cash is safe. Every media outlet and every source of information reinforces this message. It's wrong, but it's massively counter-cultural to push back against that. The real risk for the majority of people is not being in equities".

HEADLINE: **'Stock Market Crashes!!'**
Fear sells. All financial news is garbage and should be avoided. The news gives us a massively false sense that investing is risky and *"not for you!"* Probably the easiest behaviour hack any of us can employ is to stop reading financial 'news'.

Despite what we are led to believe, investing for wealth is very simple and can involve just two assets: Equities and Bonds.

Assets is the overall term used to describe different things such as Equities, Bonds, cash, property, oil, gold, etc. We focus on Equities and Bonds as they are easily investible and more accessible than other assets.

Equities aka Stocks aka Shares (all the same thing) are traded on the stock market and are shares in a company e.g. Google, Apple. The value of Equities, or the purchase price, reflects the value of the business and will increase as the business becomes bigger and more profitable. **This is how we make money.**

Bonds are loans to Government & Companies with a set term e.g. £100 for 10 years at 2% pa return. The value of Bonds, or the purchase price, will increase and decrease depending on changes in worldwide interest rates and economic changes.

The value of Equities & Bonds (i.e. the purchase price) can go up as well as down due to political or economic changes (e.g. Covid); Equities more so than Bonds as they are more volatile e.g. a stock market 'crash' is when the purchase prices of all Equities fall.

As well as the value/purchase price variance, Equities pay annual dividends to their holders depending on how successful the business year has been. Bonds pay a guaranteed interest payment every year which is set at the start of the term of the Bond.

These dividends and interest payments are paid into your investment fund, growing your returns and giving compound interest growth year on year. **This is how we make money**.

Equities provide higher returns than Bonds because businesses tend to grow in value and Bonds remain the same. But Equities are more volatile i.e. regular big ups and big downs in the value/purchase price.

Bonds provide lower returns but with reduced risk and volatility i.e. lower ups and downs.

This is why we buy both Equities and Bonds. Equities and Bonds have low correlation i.e. when Equities go down in value; Bonds tend to go up, and vice versa. By investing in a mixture of Equities and Bonds you can smooth the ups and downs.

Asset allocation refers to the mix of assets (Equities and Bonds) you hold. A sound asset allocation strategy ensures your investment portfolio is **diversified** thus spreading risk and reducing volatility. The asset allocation ratio/mix depends on two things: How long you have to invest and how much risk you can tolerate.

With a long time horizon for investing you can afford to ride the ups and downs and have a higher proportion of Equities. As the time horizon gets shorter, it is best to move to more Bonds.

Between 1984 and 2019 the FTSE 100 rose by 654% in price and 1377% on a total return basis i.e. including dividends.
On an annualised basis, this amounts to an annual price return of 5.8% and an annual total return of 7.8%......
But with volatility i.e. + or - 20% some years.

Long-term trend of FTSE All Share (1920-2013)

Risk is Volatility. This is why we buy and hold; to avoid selling in fear when the market drops and selling low, or buying in greed when the market is rising and buying high. This is why Equity Investing is for the long term...you only lose money if you sell in a downturn!

The graph below shows the FTSE All Share Index in 2020 displaying a big market fall but also a reasonably quick 'almost' recovery.

When the market started to rise, the financial news headlines were spreading fear of a '2 year recession' or 'double dip' and 'W shaped recovery'. Many investors sold when the market started to fall in early March and then missed the rise later in March. The people that sold are probably still out of the market wondering when to get back in.

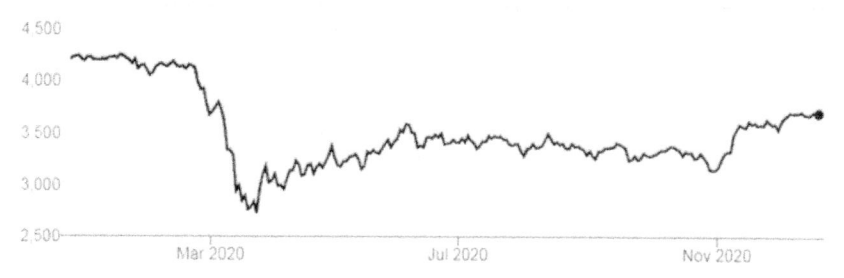

In hindsight we would have sold in February and moved back in during March – hindsight is great! That's why we buy and hold!

An investment fund is a collective purchase of assets allowing investors like you to buy into the fund and thus buy a basket of assets more easily than you could purchase them individually.

A managed investment fund or mutual fund is where assets are chosen by a manager, usually with a higher annual charge to you.

An Index investment fund does not have a manager choosing assets; it simply invests in every equity or bond in an index, providing diversification at a lower cost to you.

An index example is the FTSE 100 which is the 100 biggest companies in the UK stock market, or The S&P 500 which is the 500 biggest companies in the US stock market. A global index can contain Equities or Bonds from markets all over the world.

Low Cost: This is important. Whenever you invest in a fund, the provider makes a charge which in the past could have been anywhere up to 2 or 3%. Imagine if your fund is returning 6% and then you lose 3% of this in fees!

Today, you should not be paying more than 0.5% at most. Always check - particularly your company pension fund.

Invest in a low-cost, global, passive (i.e. not managed), index fund. This spreads your money over literally '000's of businesses across the globe for greater diversification.

Rather than relying on fund managers to pick individual shares or bonds they think are going to do well, index funds 'track' the overall performance of an entire market index, and because they typically have lower fees, you keep more of your returns - which can really add up in the long run.

Buying and holding a portfolio of passively-managed index funds will reduce market risk, cost less, and yield greater returns over time thanks to value/purchase price growth, dividends/interest, and the Magic of Compound Interest.

This Will Make You Wealthy!

WHERE TO INVEST

Investment platforms enable you to buy and hold a range of investments in one place and are designed for those making their own investment decisions. Investment platforms allow you to put your investments inside a tax-efficient wrapper - normally a stocks and shares ISA, LISA, or a self-invested personal pension (SIPP).

Vanguard is a leading example of the no-frills approach. It offers a limited range of funds, primarily index funds, in exchange, it charges extremely low fees.

Alternatively, lots of brokers provide access to a universe of funds alongside investment research and analytical tools to help you make decisions on which funds to buy e.g. AJ Bell Youinvest, Hargreaves Lansdown, Interactive Investor, and Fidelity.

Robo-advisers offer a halfway house by assessing your attitude to risk and your investment aims to recommend a tailored portfolio of funds: equities and bonds. Established providers include Nutmeg, Wealthify, and Wealthsimple.

Vanguard (www.vanguardinvestor.co.uk) was founded primarily to provide low-cost passive index funds for the general public. When you go to the website you will find all the funds listed and more details when you dive into the fund. Each fund has a NAV Price (Net asset value) which represents a fund's per share market value which is quoted on the stock market. The important point is that you do not have to buy a whole share – you can now invest in small amounts and buy portions of a share. For example, you can invest £50 per month into the Vanguard Lifestrategy 20% equity fund even though the NAV price is £171.49.

HOW TO INVEST

Option 1: One Fund. Very simple, set and forget

Option 1 is specifically designed for investing towards a pension in a Personal Pension or SIPP. It is very simple and requires no involvement from you – set and forget.

The simple option is to use a **Target Date Retirement Fund**. This provides a balance of Global Equities and Bonds where the balance of Equity and Bonds change automatically over time i.e. more bonds as you get closer to retirement.

You never need do anything. Set up your monthly Direct Debit, turn your chair sideways, look out the window and do nothing else!

You can find an example of this on the Vanguard website (If you are investing in a Company Pension Scheme make sure your money is invested in a similar fund and make sure the charges are low).

Option 2: One Fund. Simple set and check occasionally

Option 2 is for building wealth in a Pension or ISA and is still relatively simple – set and check now and again.

Investing to build wealth using a **fixed ratio Equity:Bond fund**. These provide a balance of global Equities and global Bonds where the ratio is maintained constantly. You can choose an Equity/Bond balance depending on the 'risk' you are willing to take: 100/0, 80/20, 60/40, 40/60, 20/80 and then change to different balances when you wish, or even hold multiple funds.

You can find an example of this on the Vanguard website under the name of **LifeStrategy funds**.

Option 3: Two Funds. A little more involved

Option 3 is for building wealth in a Pension or ISA and also for post-retirement when you are spending your funds.

Option 3 involves using separate asset funds in the understanding that Equity provides higher returns than Bonds, but with higher risk and volatility. With a long time horizon, you can afford to ride the short term ups and downs with a higher proportion of Equity.

For example, have a Global Equity fund **and** a Global Bond fund to a balance you decide, and then manage them over time choosing your own weighting.

You can find an example of these funds on the Vanguard website under the name of **The Vanguard FTSE Global All Cap Index Fund and The Vanguard Global Bond Index Fund.**

This option would require regular **rebalancing** i.e. buying and selling portions of your portfolio in order to set the weight of each asset class back to its original state as assets grow/fall; sell high, buy low! Also, rebalancing to adjust the weightings to fulfill a new asset allocation, if your circumstances change.

Holding separate funds has the advantage of being able to take money out of your investment account without having to sell at a loss. If you need to withdraw money for a planned event, e.g. new car; if Equity is down, Bonds are likely to be up, so you can take from the Bonds……..and vice versa.

You could also use sub sets of Equities and Bonds, and other asset classes – see part two if you want more!

THE F.I.R.E MOVEMENT
(Financial Independence Retire Early - retire early is optional!)

This is your end goal. To be able to live off the income from your investment portfolio without the need to work or with the freedom to do whatever type of work you want to do without worrying about the salary it pays.

Simply put, the goal of the FI movement is to save 25 times your annual expenses. This is also known as 'The 4% Rule': 4% being the amount, inflation linked, you can withdraw from your portfolio without running out of money over a 30 year time period in 90% of historical models.

So, if you want an income of £20,000, increasing with inflation each year, you will need a starting portfolio of £500,000 (£20,000 x 25; 4% of £500,000). The portfolio structure to achieve this is based around 50/50 Equity/Bonds.

In the UK we are lucky to still get a state pension which is approx. £8,000 pa. So, for a couple receiving a state pension of £16,000 and a required income of £20,000 at retirement, the portfolio can be reduced to £100,000.

We talked earlier about saving 20% of your income, but this is not a 'hard and fast' rule. Some proponents of the FIRE movement save up to 50% of their income to achieve financial independence within 15 years!

There are many calculators on the internet that can help you work out how much you need to save each month to get to a specified lump sum in a specified number of years, or how long it will take to reach FI if you save a specific amount every month.

PROTECT – Your family & your wealth

There are many stories of individuals or whole families having their lives turned upside down by one small slip that they could not recover from. Bad debt was discussed earlier and the compound effect of not paying it off, **in full** immediately, or as soon as possible.

This section covers some of the tools that can be used to protect you and your family against disaster.

Insurance is designed to get you back into something like the position you were in before the insured event happened. Insurance is a funny thing; you pay it, hoping you never need it, but when you do need to claim, you are very glad you have it.

Life Insurance does what it says on the tin. Term Insurance is the cheapest, for example, it guarantees to pay £10,000 anytime in the next 10 years if you die.

Critical Illness Insurance pays out a tax-free lump sum if you are diagnosed with an insured medical condition during the term of the policy. Often these are not life-ending, but they will likely mean an extended period off work.

Income Protection Insurance pays you an agreed portion of your salary each month if you cannot work because you have had an accident, fallen sick, or lost your job through no fault of your own.

A Will is a legal document that sets out your wishes regarding the distribution of your assets and the care of any children. If you die without a will, those wishes may not be carried out and your heirs may be forced to spend additional time, money, and emotional energy to settle your affairs.

A Power of Attorney is just as important as a will. Without a power of attorney, if you lose your faculties through dementia, a stroke, or accident, sorting your finances is less clear-cut than if you had died. Do not assume relatives can walk into the bank and access your money, not even to pay for your care or the mortgage.

Home Insurance covers the building that you live in, and the contents, against theft and damage by fire and flood amongst other things. Depending on your preferences, you can get cover for either or both of these at the same time. It is not a legal requirement to insure your home, but it can pay out huge amounts to cover damages caused by fire, theft, and flood damage. When you take out a mortgage most lenders insist you have a building insurance policy for the property you are buying.

Deciding how much insurance you need is like deciding on the length of a piece of string. If you are lucky, your employer will cover some of these within your employment package. Find out what they cover and decide how much extra you need. A bit like an emergency fund, work out what is right for you and your family.

Success with money can be guaranteed.

Financial success is guaranteed if you follow three simple steps:

1. SAVE – Spend less than you earn, pay yourself first & automate

2. INVEST – Be effective, keeping costs and tax low

3. PROTECT – Your family & your wealth

Saving is the area you can impose the most control over. Even those who are F.I and enjoying their money need to exercise control over their spending. For those who are building wealth, it really is the most powerful lever you can pull.

Start as soon as you can and commit to increasing your savings rate regularly. Thanks to the power of compound interest, increasing your savings rate by just £5 per week and investing in Equity, will increase your retirement pot by £55,000.

Don't save what's left over after spending; spend what's left over after saving. Pay yourself first and automate by direct debit as much as possible. Know your budget.

Spend intentionally; do not succumb to lifestyle creep or debt. Boost your income by creating passive income.

Investing effectively means buying a balance of Equities and Bonds in global index funds, wrapped inside Pensions and ISAs. Keeping costs low, using tax breaks, buy and hold for the long term. Don't meddle or try to time the markets.

Small incrementals make a difference. If you are investing £200 per month into equity, and you can reduce costs by ½%, this could add £75,000 to your pension pot.

Insuring against disaster takes care of the stuff you can't control and could have an impact on your family's financial future. Dying early or being unable to work due to accident or illness can have implications, but those implications can be mitigated to some degree by planning ahead.

Do these things and you are guaranteed success. Not rocket science is it? And yet we are not taught any of this, and because there are so many other pressures on us, it is easy to fail.

Actually, it should be encouraging that it really is this simple - literally anyone can do it.

Yes, it is harder if you are on a low income, or you are a single parent, or you have a disability……but it is still possible.

Financial success is there for the taking - will you grab hold?

THE END…………..

BUT, If you would like to understand more…..read on!

The Secret to Financial Success:
Part 2

It is not *all about the money, money, money!*

Health, Wealth, and Happiness. These are the areas you should focus on to improve your life for the better.
Work on these and you will live a more balanced lifestyle, become a well-rounded person, ultimately leading to you being happy and successful!

Positive Mental Attitude: Can do rather than can't do

Set Goals: If you have no goals then you have nothing to achieve

Set short term and long term goals   Fail to plan. Plan to fail

Nobody's perfect. Learn from mistakes

Be Curious: Keep Learning

Lifestyle: These things all help to improve your PMA and general wellbeing:

Exercise - gym, running, walking in the countryside, team sports

Stretch - your mind and body every day (before and after exercise)

Food - Good healthy food and fun food in moderation
                              Water - Keep hydrated

Sleep - aim for 8 hours a day. You will feel fresher, more alive, and cognitively better

Behavioural finance and investor bias

'Stock Market Crashes!!'

Fight or flight?
We are naturally wired to buy when Equities are high and to sell when they fall. This is intuitive...but it is wrong! Unfortunately, fear of loss is greater than pleasure from gains.

If you sell when Equities fall, you are locking in a loss.
If you then wait for Equities to rise before getting back in, you are locking in another loss! This is how most investors operate – timing the market. It is hardwired into our human DNA.

If the price of a dress/steak/car is offered on sale at half price, we rush to buy. If the stock market crashes by 50%, do we rush to buy or cry SELL!! Put it another way, do you wait for the price of housing to go down before you buy a house?

Volatility and risk disappear if you look over the long term. Investing in globally diverse, low-cost index funds is for the long term growth of your wealth.

From the famous words of one of the most esteemed investors in history Warren Buffett, to be a successful investor:

"Be Fearful When Others Are Greedy and Greedy When Others Are Fearful"

If you have a long time frame and are investing in your Equity portfolio every month, would you stop the direct debit if the market crashes overnight? **NO!** The stock market will bounce back and you are in the fantastic position of continuing to buy when it is on sale!

If you are fearful and could not stomach a 30% fall in your Equity portfolio, this is where an allocation in Bonds will help calm the nerves.

Buy and hold, or *set and forget* investing is easy – too easy! People think they should work hard, study hard, play the market, etc. to make money.
Again, it is counter-intuitive to do nothing and win!

While active investors will tell you it's possible to time the market and make a killing by playing stocks, the data seems to show otherwise.

Fidelity conducted an internal study — a performance review of accounts between 2003 and 2013 to find which accounts did the best. They found that the best performing accounts were investors who were DEAD! In second place were investors who had FORGOTTEN they had accounts at Fidelity.
Set and forget investing is probably the easiest and safest bet for beginner investors anyway.

A common mantra in investing is **'time in the market, not timing the market'**. In other words, the best way to make money is to get in and stay invested in the market for the long term and take advantage of compound interest. Jumping in and out of the market and trying to time ups and downs rarely works out well.

Buy & Hold. Set & Forget.

Pension V ISA

Start early and save often is the most effective way of bringing the pot at the end of the rainbow within reach. Both pension and ISA wrappers encourage you to save by offering generous tax relief, but this comes at different times and with different trade-offs.

A pension allows you to make payments before tax – in other words, you do not pay tax that would otherwise be due on the bit of income you have put aside. For a basic rate taxpayer, that is 20% of the whole amount before tax which the taxman will add to your pension. If you are a higher earner, you can claim a further 20% or 25% back through your tax return. Also, many employers will match your contributions, which is effectively 'free money' that you should take advantage of before investing elsewhere.

By contrast, payments into an ISA attract no tax relief. The ISA comes into its own when you want to spend your savings. All payments from an ISA are tax-free.
With a pension, you can only take out 25% of your fund free of tax, with any further payments attracting income tax at your normal rate.

A Pension can only be cashed in after the age of 55. An ISA can be cashed in at any time. Therefore an ISA can provide a tax-efficient home for savings when you are young or your income is unpredictable and you need reassurance that the money will be available at short notice if needed.

The Lifetime ISA (LISA) is a special offer not to be missed. The Lifetime ISA lets you save up to £4,000 every tax year towards a first home or your retirement, with the state adding a 25% bonus on top of what you save. That means you could get a chunky £1,000 of free cash annually. Plus, you earn interest on whatever you save, and as it's an ISA, that interest is tax-free.

You can withdraw the money at any time to buy a house without any penalties. You can withdraw the money at any time after the age of 60 without any penalties. But, if you withdraw before the age of 60, not for house purchase, there is a 25% charge.

You can pay up to £40,000 per year into a pension, capped at your earnings or £3,600 if you do not earn anything.

You can hold both an ISA and a LISA at the same time; the maximum that you can pay is £20,000 per year.

Passive investing

Passive investing is all about investing in low cost index funds for the long term. No active management. Buy and hold.

LOW COST

If you invest in an ISA or Pension via the Vanguard platform (www.vanguardinvestor.co.uk), the charges you pay are kept very low. The average fund management charge is 0.20% p.a. The annual account fee is 0.15% p.a. This is a total annual cost of just 0.35% p.a.

Some platforms/funds charge anywhere between 1% and 2%. Saving 1% in fees may not sound much, but it is more than most savings accounts currently pay and can make a huge difference.

If you are investing £200 per month over a 40 year working lifetime, assuming an equity return of 7% is reduced by 1% in fees, this would reduce your retirement pot by £125,000!

<u>GLOBAL</u> INDEX

The Vanguard FTSE Global All Cap Index Fund – accumulation* seeks diversification (spreading the risk and volatility) by tracking the performance of The FTSE Global All Cap Index** and investing in a representative sample of shares. It does this by actually buying and holding shares in 6,816 companies across the world. There is no manager choosing which shares are the best shares to buy.

The 6,816 shares are bought from stock markets across the world depending on the size of those markets. USA is the largest of the markets and comprises 57% of the shares. Japan is the next largest at 7%. The UK is just 4%.

The global fund is also spread across all the different sectors of the market: technology, financial, industrial, consumer, health, etc.

Vanguard maintains the balance of the fund always at the same specified proportions regardless of markets and sectors ups and downs - effectively selling high and buying low.

The Vanguard Global Bond Index Fund seeks to track an index fund of global government, government-related agencies, and corporate bonds from around the world with maturities greater than one year and incorporates 12,643 bonds.

The Vanguard Target Retirement Funds and The Vanguard Lifestrategy Funds incorporate both Equity and Bond global index trackers.

*Accumulation means that company dividends are paid back into the fund rather than being paid out as income to you.
**The FTSE Global All Cap Index is comprised of large, mid-sized and small company shares in developed and emerging markets around the world.

Target Date Retirement funds

Vanguard's Target Date Retirement funds are ready-made portfolios that make investing for retirement easy. You simply choose a fund based on when you plan to retire and then let it run.

Vanguard's low fees ensure that any returns you receive over the decades during which you invest are not gobbled up by a fund manager.

The fund's aim is to balance the risk needed to grow wealth while also taking steps to preserve retirement savings. At the start, they invest your money mostly in Equities, because although Equities are riskier, they offer higher potential returns. As you get closer to retirement, it starts switching out of higher-risk, higher-reward Equities and into more stable Bonds.

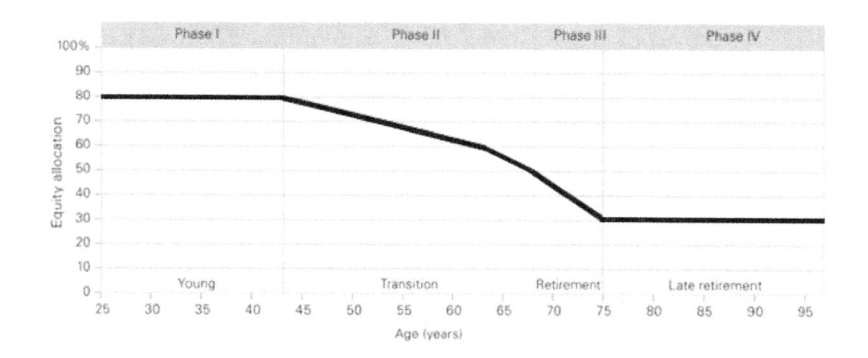

Vanguard automatically keeps to the right balance of Equities and Bonds depending on how far you are from retirement.

At a young age, with time on your side, you can ride out any ups and downs in the stock market. As you get closer to retirement, the gradual move into Bonds provides more stability, but offers lower potential returns.

The idea is that as you get closer to your goal, you will be more interested in preserving what you have with Bonds, rather than making big potential gains with Equities. After all, you do not want a stock market slump to reduce your savings just before you intend to start using them, as you won't have time to regain any losses.

For the UK version of the Target Retirement Funds, the portfolio has been tweaked to be more UK biased as shown below:

Funds	Year 1	Year 50
Equity UK	20%	10%
Equity Global excl UK	60%	20%
Bonds UK	5%	30%
Bonds Global excl UK	15%	50%

Fixed ratio Equity/Bond funds

Vanguard offers five LifeStrategy funds which are fixed at Equity/Bond split; 20%, 40%, 60%, 80% or 100% Equity. Fees are very low; a total annual cost of just 0.37% means that if you invest £10,000 you will pay Vanguard £37 each year.

Each LifeStrategy fund holds 6,000 to 20,000 Equities and Bonds from around the world, helping to reduce risk. Vanguard monitors each LifeStrategy fund to make sure it sticks to the original balance of Equities and Bonds; this gives you the ability to decide which balance best fits your investment goal and attitude to risk.

Your Pension is a long term investment, so the opportunity is there to start with an Equity heavy portfolio (100% Equity) and reduce the risk as time goes by:
- Pension early years 100% Equity.
- Pension later years – stop buying 100% and move to 60%, 40%...

Your ISA could be split into two portfolios:
- Long term equity heavy portion e.g. 100% Equity.
- Short term (i.e. for future purchases) in 80% Bonds.
- One Equity fund and one Bond fund so that you can withdraw from either depending on performance: if Equity is down, withdraw from Bonds, and vice versa.

Lifestrategy funds have a home bias in comparison to the actual global equity market i.e. there is a higher percentage of UK Equity and less US Equity.

What is the best balance of Equities and Bonds

Let's look at the effects of different Equity/Bond splits over the last thirty years. The data in the table is from 1986 to 2015. Equity is represented by the S&P 500 Index and Bonds represented by five-Year US Treasury Notes:

(Remember, past performance is not indicative of future returns).

	Annualized Return	Standard Deviation	Growth of $100,000
100% Stock	10.37%	15.22%	$ 1,928,737.00
80% Stock 20% Bond	9.77%	12.17%	$ 1,640,004.00
60% Stock 40% Bond	9.06%	9.23%	$ 1,349,504.00
40% Stock 60% Bond	8.24%	6.54%	$ 1,075,423.00
20% Stock 80% Bond	7.31%	4.59%	$ 830,475.00

Standard deviation helps determine market volatility or the spread of asset prices from their average price. When prices move wildly, standard deviation is high, meaning an investment will be risky. Low standard deviation means prices are calm, so investments come with low risk.

You will see that the rate of return increases as the proportion of Equities increase. You will also see that the size of the ups and downs increases as the proportion of Equities increase.

The more Equity you have in your portfolio, the more money you're likely to have when you retire, but you need to be able to stick it out through some pretty rough patches to get those long-term returns.

Between March 2008-February 2009, the 100% Equity portfolio lost over 43% of its value. Even the 60% Equity portfolio lost over a quarter of its value in that same twelve month period.

Between 2000 and 2002 (the aftermath of the Tech Bubble), the S&P 500 Index lost almost 38% of its value. Not as much as in 2008, but it was more spread out – the pain lasted three times as long and it was difficult for many investors to stay disciplined.

To get higher returns from Equity you need to be able to stay put even during the ugly times. Investing is about meeting your financial goals 30 years in the future, not getting the high score for this year, so making your portfolio match your risk tolerance is key to staying disciplined. You can work out your risk tolerance using internet tools – see the Vanguard website for example.

The 60:40 (Equities:Bonds) portfolio is agreed to be the happy medium of investing portfolios. Its tilt towards Equities makes it pro-growth, but the significant slug in Bonds provides welcome relief during crashes when other investors flee to safer assets.

Of course, all the figures discussed earlier are historical and cannot be relied on to happen in the future. Due to the low interest rates currently from Bonds, some believe that the 60/40 fund will not make these kinds of returns in the future. There is also some worry that Bonds do not offer as much diversification or negative correlation from Equities as in the past. Other asset classes could be used, but these bring their own risk.

Passive investing does not have to be complicated

Most investors eventually conclude that complexity only offers the illusion of sophistication and they are actually better off keeping things simple. There is a mountain of evidence showing that passive investing is a superior strategy compared to believing that the latest hot fund manager or investment scheme will smash the market. Use low-cost, global index trackers to reap the market returns and get rich slowly. It is as simple as investing gets.

With passive investing, you don't worry about what the price of gold is doing this week, nor do you worry about 'stock market crashes' or 'rallies'. There is no need to 'time the market', pick winning companies, or convince yourself that you have special powers to beat other investors – especially since the vast army of superbly equipped professionals cannot reliably outperform either.

As long term passive investors we don't worry about short term volatility. If you don't think you can withstand potentially large short term falls in the value of your portfolio, or you are ready to spend some of your portfolio, use a Bond cushion.

You can get by with just one low cost global index fund of Equity and Bonds. Two funds give the ability to withdraw cash if needed from whichever fund is appreciating, avoiding selling at a loss.

Or, you can diversify across a number of asset classes or even sub sets of asset classes as described next.

Passive investing can be complicated, if you want!

Alternative asset classes to Equity and Bonds can be used to spread risk and reduce volatility. The asset universe is extremely broad and these are just a few examples of some that can be used to diversify a portfolio:

Equity and Bonds can be broken down into many subsets with the aim of producing returns greater than the equity market or bond market as a whole. For example; small cap, value, growth, short term bonds, junk bonds, etc. (Global index funds cover <u>all</u> market sectors, geographical sectors, and subsets such as these).

Infrastructure is popular when governments looking to reboot economies are investing, for example, in renewable energy. An attraction of infrastructure is that returns are broadly reliable; often inflation linked to 20 or 30 year government contracts.

Real estate is lowly correlated with equities but highly correlated with the economic environment. The collapse of Arcadia and Debenhams serves as a reminder of the risk.

Gold is often the panic asset of choice and has done very well during the coronavirus crisis. It can be used in a portfolio as an insurance policy in times of stress but is extremely volatile.

Model portfolios have been constructed using alternative assets to show how different balances of asset classes can maximise returns, reduce volatility, or a mixture of both when measured against historical data. Examples include the All-Weather Portfolio, Permanent Portfolio, Golden Butterfly, and Couch Potato.

The idea is that by diversifying across a number of asset classes you will always have at least one asset that performs in every economic environment short of the apocalypse, but different balances will have different results. For example:

- Equities and property for growth.
- Government bonds (and cash) for recessions.
- Inflation-resistant bonds for high inflation conditions.
- Gold for inflation and when nothing else works.

This is still **Passive Investing**, using index funds and no active management, just more asset classes. Buy and hold, rebalance annually.

When you mix these assets or subsets of assets together, the sum of the total portfolio can be greater than the parts. For example, mixing two or more volatile assets in a portfolio can reduce the overall volatility depending on the asset correlation.

You can have two 60/40 portfolios of Equities/Bonds, but by breaking down those two assets in different ways, you will get different results when analysed against historical data.

These model portfolios of mixed assets help an investor to decide how much risk they are prepared to take to gain higher level of returns.

Take the year 2020 as an example of a <u>very</u> volatile year with worldwide stock markets falling by 20-30% in a matter of days due to covid fears, but bouncing back very quickly. The Vanguard Total World Index fund returned 13.4% but with a standard deviation of 27.5%. The FTSE all share index finished the year down 10%. Other assets like gold and bonds increased in value as the stock market fell. Keep in mind that you can't judge investment strategies by a single year:

- The Couch Potato portfolio returned 15% for a 12% standard deviation. This portfolio consists of 50% S&P 500 and 50% 20+year long term US treasuries.

- The Permanent portfolio had a low risk standard deviation of 7.8% and returned 13% (this strategy usually returns 5%-7%). The portfolio consists of 25% each of US large cap stocks, US long-term bonds, US short-term bonds, and gold.

If you do set up a portfolio of mixed assets, you will have to choose a balance e.g. 50% Equity: 50% Bonds, and then maintain this by **Rebalancing**. Often the only time people wonder whether they should have rebalanced is after a big stock market downturn. If you have diversified your portfolio into different assets to reduce volatility and improve risk/return characteristics, it makes no sense to abandon this just because one asset class has boomed and another slumped.

Periodically rebalancing your portfolio by selling down winning assets to buy more underperforming assets can boost your returns. It keeps volatility closer to your tolerance levels and reduces the risk of your portfolio being exposed to bubble markets.

Bucket structure for F.I.

Once you have achieved F.I and are living off your portfolio, you will need to plan how best to drawdown from your assets.

One way forward is to use *The Bucket Strategy:* three separate holdings based on the withdrawal time horizon. The aim being to avoid market timing i.e. having to sell assets when they are down.

Bucket 1 holds cash for short-term withdrawals - anywhere from six months to two years' worth of cash to live on. Cash that you can draw upon when it is not a good time to sell Equity. Having this cash buffer provides peace of mind; you shouldn't be rattled during periods of short-term market turbulence, because spending will be relatively undisturbed and the rest of the portfolio can recover when the market eventually does.

Bucket 2 consists primarily of Bonds that offer higher long-term returns than cash with much lower volatility than Equity - up to eight years' worth of portfolio withdrawals.

Bucket 3 is the long term component in Equities, offering higher potential returns than buckets 1 or 2 but with higher expected volatility.

This portfolio is designed to be customised based on your own expected withdrawal rate. For example, following the 4% rule, someone withdrawing £20,000 from a portfolio of £500,000 could earmark £40,000 in cash (two years' worth of withdrawals), £160,000 in bonds (eight years' worth of withdrawals), and the remaining £300,000 in stocks.

This gives a 60/40 portfolio: 60% Equity with 40% Bonds/cash.

Alternatively, buckets 2 & 3 can be set at a lower level of risk. For example, bucket 1 is still £40,000 in cash, buckets 2 and 3 are set at 60% Equity and 40% Bonds, which is £184,000 Bond in bucket 2 and £276,000 Equity in bucket 3. This could be slightly less volatile but could have a slightly lower return.

Maintenance:
When bucket 1 needs topping up, take out of buckets 2 and 3 and rebalance the funds to the desired weighting. Rebalancing involves trimming appreciated assets and using the proceeds for living expenses. Of course, there are those years when almost nothing performs especially well; 2018 was a recent example. This is a key reason for holding a cash bucket; it provides a buffer if nothing is ripe for pruning. Spend the cash bucket and refill it when Equities and/or Bonds recover.

This underscores the importance of drawdown portfolios incorporating separate holdings rather than all-in-one funds like Target Retirement or Lifestrategy funds.

You will also need to consider how you want your portfolio's assets balance to change over time. You may not want your asset allocation to remain static throughout retirement. You may want to become more conservative or even more aggressive. Knowing this at the outset can help determine how you rebalance your portfolio and what you do with excess funds above and beyond what you need for living expenses.

On an annual basis, record cash flow forecast against actual, and track the portfolio value over time to ensure it stays on track. Keep a record of the portfolio asset mix so that you know when to rebalance. Remember to consider other items that can be included in your net worth calculation and how these will affect your cash flow and withdrawal rate going forward. For example, the value of property you own and future state pension.

Avoid paying Income Tax by withdrawing from a mix of ISA (no Income tax) and Pension (pay income tax above the personal tax-free allowance at 20%). By taking money out of pensions using UFPLS, you can take up to £16,000 P/A tax-free. Above this, you would pay 20% in tax.

What if you reach F.I / retirement with your pension in a Target Date Retirement Fund?

In this case, your portfolio balance may be 80/20 in favour of Bonds and this balance is unlikely to maintain the 4% rule.
You may not need to maintain the 4% rule if you have saved more than 25x required income, and if you leave the portfolio as it is, and the stock market crashes, you would not be greatly affected.
You could have a separate ISA in Equities, and this would help with tax reduction as well.

Numerous withdrawal strategies can be utilised. You may be able to manage this yourself, if not, employ a financial planner to devise a plan (NOT move your funds to their 'recommended funds').

Financial plan

How and when each of us achieves FI will depend on many variables such as income, savings rate, investment return, time, etc.
Sitting down and making a financial plan will help to identify what you want to achieve and then detail how to get there.

The three key elements to a financial plan are:
- Financial goals.
- Budget & saving strategy.
- Investment strategy.

What is your current financial situation?
What are your short term financial goals?
What are your medium/long term financial goals?
What emergency fund requirement do you have?
What % of your income are you prepared to save?
Where will you be allocating the money (Pension/LISA/ISA)?
What are your target allocation and types of funds?
How old do you want to be when you reach FI?
How much money do you need to live on comfortably?
What drawdown plan will you use in FI?
What reasons would you consider changing your financial plan?

These are just some basic questions to ask yourself to help create your financial plan. Keep it simple, one or two A4 sheets at most so that you can refer to it and 'keep it alive'.

The very first chapter in this book covered the importance of having a written budget and savings strategy. Knowing exactly where your money is going: how you will split your income to cover essentials, non-essentials, and saving/investment. Save more than you spend, automate as many payments as possible and pay yourself first – this is the bedrock of your financial plan.

Your investment strategy will detail the accounts and funds you will use, the level of risk you are prepared to take, and the balance of assets you will use.

It is incredibly powerful to go through the process of actually writing down a financial plan, particularly the investment strategy. Some investors have a game plan for investing 'in their head', but when times get tough and emotions start to interfere, the financial plan will help you to buy and hold, rebalance, keep your head when all about you are losing theirs!

Your investment strategy will be a guiding light when the markets do something you aren't expecting. By not using a written plan, you are more likely to be short-term focused and chase near-term performance.

By working on a financial plan, you are helping ensure that you remain focused on achieving the right goals.

Writing it down, of course, is not the end of the process. It is important to regularly review, modify the plan as necessary, and continually check-in to make sure your actions are lining up with your plan.

Practical example

Current financial position:
Dave leaves college with a £1,000 debt (Remember, student loan is not a debt – it is a tax on future income) and no savings. He gets his first job paying £25,000 per annum. Happy Days!

What are Dave's goals?

- Use the 50/30/20 rule to define a budget.
- Pay off the £1,000 loan a.s.a.p. then build an emergency fund.
- Maximise the employer contribution in the company pension.
- Budget for 2x two week holidays annually.
- Start saving for a new home in 4 years' time.
- Reach FI by age 55.

Dave's employer provides a company pension and takes the contribution gross i.e. before tax. They also match Dave's payment up to 5%. Dave is definitely taking advantage of this free money and will pay 5% of his gross income with the aim of increasing it later. Dave pays 5% or £104 each month (no tax paid) into his pension and the employer doubles this!
(*By making the payment a % rather than £ value, the amount will increase as the salary increases over time. Good Move!*).

Taking account of the pension payment, gross pay is now £23,750 and take-home pay (after income tax, student loan tax, and national insurance) is £19,800 or £1,650 per month.

Using the 50/30/20 rule to define a budget, the monthly amounts are:

1. 50% of income should cover fixed costs/essentials £825
2. 30% of income covers none essentials £495
3. 20% save/invest. Pay yourself first automatically £330

(5% or £104 in pension already. So £100 could be diverted to one of the other pots..?).

Dave's budget spreadsheet shows that his fixed costs/essentials come to £850 per month. He decides to take £25 from his none essentials pot leaving £470 to spend monthly on none essentials.

The £850 fixed costs/essentials are either paid by monthly direct debit from his current account or left in his current account to cover annual expenses – all except food and petrol.

The £470 goes into a contact card account to spend daily.
Dave also adds his monthly amount budgeted for food and petrol into this account as these are day to day expenses.

All Done. Dave just has to ensure his contact card account stays in credit every month. Any underspend at the end of the month can move to savings to build up a seasonal buffer or for bigger annual spends. Then just keep a check on fixed costs/essentials and none essentials to make sure they don't 'lifestyle creep'!

That leaves £330 per month to save and invest – putting aside the £104 per month going into his pension.

For the first 3 months, he will use this to pay off his loan. Then for the following 3 months build an emergency fund in a high interest savings account.

Once this is accomplished, for the following 3½ years, he will pay the maximum £333 each month into a cash LISA to save for a house deposit (This is increased to £416 per month by the Government). This can also be considered part of the emergency fund as it can be accessed with a small financial penalty, if necessary.

Once the goal of buying a house is achieved, this allocation will be moved to a stocks and shares LISA/ISA alongside a review of the amount of pension payment.

What is his investment strategy?

- Do not try to time the market. Buy and hold long-term. Contribute monthly by direct debit and stick to low-cost, global index funds. Let returns compound over time.
- Aim to reach FI by age 55. Maintain a 90% stocks/10% bonds allocation. At age 45, change to 60% stocks/40% bonds. At 50, plan to shift to a bucket system.
- Rebalance annually. If asset allocations are off track by more than 5%, rebalance to get back on track.
- Account allocation; ISA/LISA/Pension.

And finally….

A STORY TO SHARE FROM THE FIRE COMMUNITY:

Exactly a year ago, I got purposeful with my money - I wasn't bad with money, but I just wasn't making progress either. I work in a charity and always thought I'd never earn much so maybe didn't need to think about money beyond covering my expenses?

But last August, I'd just been through a big break up; my friends were all getting married, leaving London and having babies; I had a new boss; both my parents were fighting cancer and I had a mystery health condition I was struggling with.... I needed some control over my life.

I cleared a £1200 balance on a credit card with some of my savings while sitting on a bus to work, and figured out what I would need in the bank as a 6 month emergency fund to make my life work if I had no income. It seemed like such a crazy amount to save up.

One year on, not only have I got there, but I am funding all my true expenses, have savings for holidays and other fun, pay 15% of my salary into my pension and have investments I'm adding to in an index fund. I've got clear money goals and honestly feel much more secure, as well as giving myself permission to enjoy (some) of my money in a way I've not done before. Next stop is to ramp up my investing and continue to work towards being the financially fierce, independent woman my future self needs, and so I can continue to do jobs I care a lot about and impact other people.

Printed in Great Britain
by Amazon